The W

Smartest

Most Hilarious

408

FACTS

YOU WILL EVER HEAR

Blow Minds, Break the Ice,
and Become the Funniest Person
in the Room (Even If You're Just Killing
Time in the Bathroom)

STOCKING STUFFERS FOR TEENS

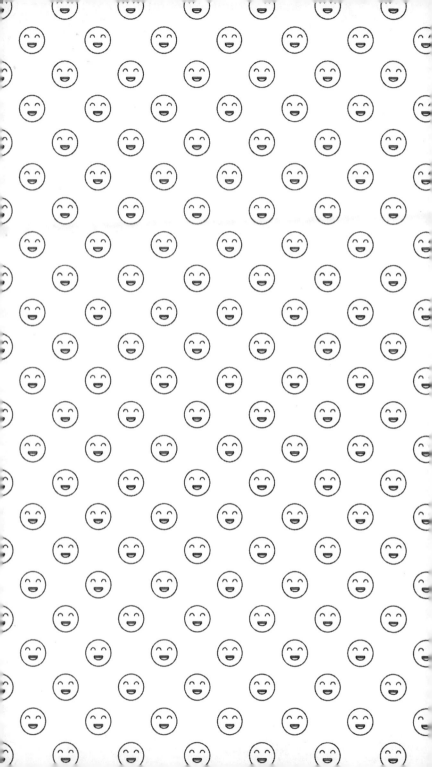

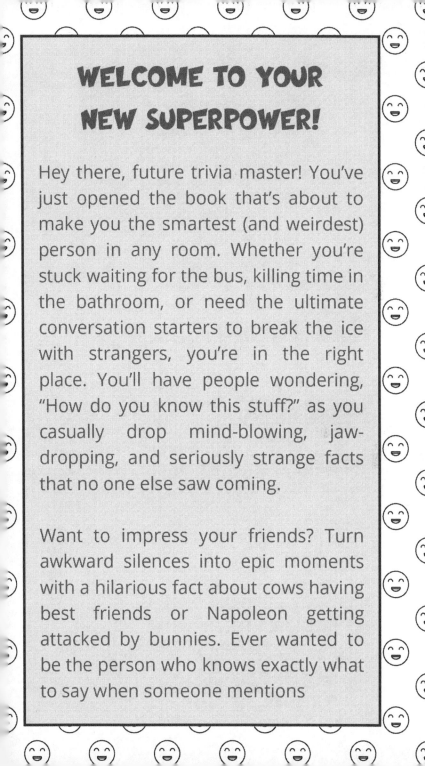

WELCOME TO YOUR NEW SUPERPOWER!

Hey there, future trivia master! You've just opened the book that's about to make you the smartest (and weirdest) person in any room. Whether you're stuck waiting for the bus, killing time in the bathroom, or need the ultimate conversation starters to break the ice with strangers, you're in the right place. You'll have people wondering, "How do you know this stuff?" as you casually drop mind-blowing, jaw-dropping, and seriously strange facts that no one else saw coming.

Want to impress your friends? Turn awkward silences into epic moments with a hilarious fact about cows having best friends or Napoleon getting attacked by bunnies. Ever wanted to be the person who knows exactly what to say when someone mentions sports, nature, history, or the human body? You're about to be that person—the one with all the bizarre, unbelievable truths that will make everyone lean in and ask, "Wait, what?"

And hey, maybe you're just here to entertain yourself while you, uh... "do your business." No judgment—this is the perfect read for those 5 (or 15) minutes of bathroom solitude. After all, why not become a human fact machine while sitting on the porcelain throne?

So dive in, laugh a little, learn a lot, and prepare to blow minds with your new arsenal of insane sports, hilarious history, nature's quirks, and wild body oddities. By the time you're done, you'll have enough random knowledge to outsmart even the know-it-alls.

SO, WHAT'S INSIDE THIS BOOK?

Inside this fact-packed book, you'll find four epic sections, each filled with 102 ridiculous, mind-blowing, and hilarious facts that will have you dropping knowledge bombs at every turn. Whether you're looking to impress your friends, kick off a random conversation, or simply entertain yourself while waiting for your food delivery, this book has it all.

In Part 1: Crazy Sports, you'll discover the wildest, most unexpected competitions that exist around the world. From Wife Carrying to Ferret Legging, you won't believe these sports are real (but they totally are!). Take this for example: In Finland, there's a Wife Carrying Championship where the grand prize is your wife's weight in beer. Yeah, that's a real thing.

Next up, Part 2: Hilarious History brings you the funniest, weirdest, and most absurd moments from the past. Did you know that Napoleon was once attacked by a mob of bunnies? Or that a man once won a horse race... after he had died? History class never covered these stories!

In Part 3: Nature Gone Nuts, get ready for the animal kingdom like you've never seen it before. From cube-shaped wombat poop to sea otters holding hands as they sleep, you'll learn that nature is full of surprises— some cute, some crazy, and all unforgettable.

And finally, Part 4: Human Body Oddities takes you deep into the strange world of the human body. Think you know your own body? Think again! Did you know you produce enough saliva in your lifetime to fill two swimming pools? Or that humans actually glow in the dark (even if it's too faint to see)? Get ready to rethink everything you thought you knew about being human.

We've made it easy for you to jump into any section, share a fact with someone nearby, and instantly become the most interesting person in the room. And hey, if you're just killing time in the bathroom, why not leave smarter than when you went in?

Once you're done blowing minds with these unbelievable truths, we'd love for you to leave us an honest review. Let the world know how this book made you laugh, scratch your head, and maybe even say, "Wait, what?!" Your feedback helps others find this treasure trove of randomness, and we can't wait to hear what you think!

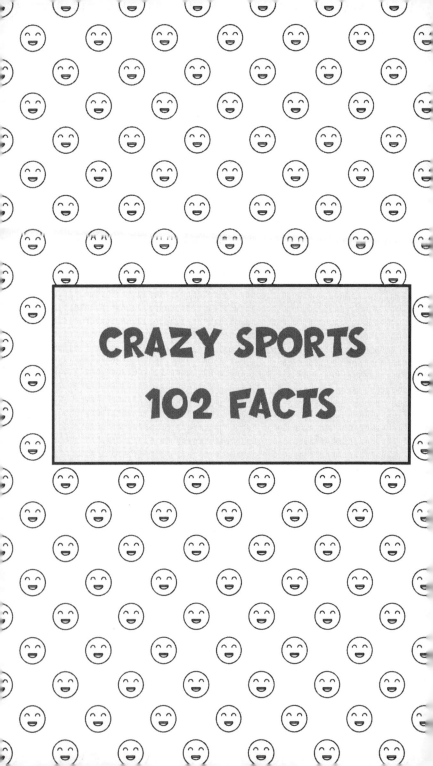

CRAZY SPORTS
102 FACTS

TUG-OF-WAR WAS AN OLYMPIC
SPORT FROM 1900 TO 1920.

IN UNDERWATER HOCKEY, PLAYERS
USE MINI STICKS TO PUSH A PUCK
ALONG THE POOL FLOOR WHILE
HOLDING THEIR BREATH.

THERE IS A WORLD GURNING
CHAMPIONSHIP WHERE PARTICIPANTS
COMPETE TO MAKE
THE UGLIEST FACE.

IN FINLAND, PEOPLE COMPETE IN A SPORT CALLED "WIFE CARRYING," WHERE THE PRIZE IS YOUR WIFE'S WEIGHT IN BEER.

CHESS BOXING IS A REAL SPORT THAT ALTERNATES BETWEEN ROUNDS OF CHESS AND BOXING.

THE WORLD TOE WRESTLING CHAMPIONSHIP HAS BEEN HELD ANNUALLY IN ENGLAND SINCE THE 1970S.

THERE'S A SPORT IN THE UK CALLED "EXTREME IRONING" WHERE PARTICIPANTS IRON CLOTHES IN THE MOST EXTREME PLACES, LIKE MOUNTAIN TOPS OR UNDERWATER.

THE LONGEST TENNIS MATCH IN HISTORY LASTED 11 HOURS AND 5 MINUTES AT WIMBLEDON IN 2010.

IN JAPAN, THERE'S A SPORT CALLED "BO-TAOSHI," WHERE TWO TEAMS OF 75 PLAYERS EACH TRY TO KNOCK DOWN THE OTHER TEAM'S POLE.

UNICYCLE HOCKEY IS EXACTLY WHAT IT SOUNDS LIKE: HOCKEY PLAYED WHILE RIDING UNICYCLES.

BUZKASHI IS THE NATIONAL SPORT OF AFGHANISTAN, WHERE PLAYERS ON HORSEBACK TRY TO GRAB A DEAD GOAT AND GET IT ACROSS THE GOAL LINE.

FERRET LEGGING IS A SPORT WHERE CONTESTANTS PUT LIVE FERRETS DOWN THEIR PANTS AND SEE HOW LONG THEY CAN ENDURE.

SEPAK TAKRAW, A POPULAR SPORT IN SOUTHEAST ASIA, IS LIKE VOLLEYBALL BUT PLAYERS USE THEIR FEET, HEAD, KNEES, AND CHEST TO HIT THE BALL.

IN COMPETITIVE SNOWBALL FIGHTING, TEAMS OF SEVEN BATTLE IT OUT WITH HUNDREDS OF SNOWBALLS IN JAPAN'S YUKIGASSEN CHAMPIONSHIPS.

IN THE UK, PEOPLE RACE DOWN A STEEP HILL CHASING A ROLLING WHEEL OF CHEESE IN THE ANNUAL COOPER'S HILL CHEESE-ROLLING EVENT.

SHIN-KICKING IS A COMPETITIVE SPORT IN WHICH TWO CONTESTANTS TRY TO KICK EACH OTHER'S SHINS UNTIL ONE FALLS OVER.

THE RED BULL CLIFF DIVING WORLD SERIES FEATURES ATHLETES DIVING FROM HEIGHTS AS TALL AS 90 FEET INTO WATER.

IN THE NETHERLANDS, PEOPLE COMPETE IN "FIERLJEPPEN," A SPORT WHERE CONTESTANTS POLE VAULT OVER CANALS.

"OSTRICH RACING" IS A COMPETITIVE EVENT IN SOME PARTS OF AFRICA AND THE UNITED STATES WHERE JOCKEYS RIDE OSTRICHES.

THERE IS A PILLOW FIGHTING WORLD CHAMPIONSHIP WHERE COMPETITORS GO HEAD-TO-HEAD IN PILLOW FIGHTS.

IN ITALY, THERE'S A SPORT CALLED "CALCIO STORICO," A BRUTAL MIX OF SOCCER, RUGBY, AND WRESTLING.

IN PROFESSIONAL ARM WRESTLING, THE WINNER IS DETERMINED NOT JUST BY STRENGTH BUT ALSO BY TECHNIQUE, INCLUDING HAND PLACEMENT AND GRIP.

CYCLE BALL, OR "RADBALL," IS LIKE SOCCER, BUT PLAYED ON BICYCLES.

THE WORLD SAUNA CHAMPIONSHIPS WERE HELD IN FINLAND UNTIL THEY WERE CANCELED IN 2010 AFTER A COMPETITOR SUFFERED SEVERE BURNS.

UNDERWATER RUGBY IS PLAYED IN A SWIMMING POOL, WITH PLAYERS COMPETING TO GET A NEGATIVELY BUOYANT BALL INTO THE OPPONENT'S GOAL.

JOGGLING IS A SPORT THAT COMBINES JOGGING AND JUGGLING.

THERE'S A 50 KM BACKWARD RACE THAT TAKES PLACE EVERY YEAR IN GERMANY.

IN RUSSIA, PEOPLE PLAY A SPORT CALLED "CAR CURLING," WHERE CARS ARE USED INSTEAD OF STONES ON AN ICE RINK.

THE CAMEL WRESTLING CHAMPIONSHIP IS A POPULAR EVENT IN TURKEY, WHERE TWO CAMELS WRESTLE EACH OTHER.

LAWN MOWER RACING INVOLVES COMPETITORS RACING MODIFIED LAWN MOWERS, AND IS POPULAR IN THE UK AND THE US.

ELEPHANT POLO IS EXACTLY WHAT IT SOUNDS LIKE: POLO PLAYED WHILE RIDING ELEPHANTS.

IN 1986, THE CHICAGO BEARS RELEASED A RAP SONG CALLED THE "SUPER BOWL SHUFFLE," WHICH ACTUALLY MADE IT TO THE BILLBOARD CHARTS.

KABADDI, A POPULAR SPORT IN INDIA, INVOLVES TEAMS TAKING TURNS SENDING A PLAYER INTO THE OPPONENT'S SIDE TO TAG AS MANY PLAYERS AS POSSIBLE AND THEN ESCAPE WITHOUT GETTING TACKLED.

DODGEBALL IS PLAYED AS A PROFESSIONAL SPORT WITH LEAGUES ACROSS THE WORLD.

EXTREME SKIING, ALSO KNOWN AS ALPINE SKIING, INVOLVES SKIING DOWN STEEP, OFTEN DANGEROUS TERRAIN.

IN JAPAN, THERE'S A SPORT CALLED "KANINHOP" OR RABBIT SHOW JUMPING, WHERE RABBITS ARE TRAINED TO HOP OVER HURDLES.

BUBBLE SOCCER IS PLAYED WITH PLAYERS ENCASED IN GIANT INFLATABLE BUBBLES, AND INVOLVES KNOCKING EACH OTHER OVER WHILE TRYING TO SCORE GOALS.

IN COMPETITIVE CHERRY PIT SPITTING, PARTICIPANTS COMPETE TO SEE WHO CAN SPIT A CHERRY PIT THE FARTHEST.

IN FINLAND, THE AIR GUITAR WORLD CHAMPIONSHIPS INVITE PEOPLE FROM ALL OVER THE WORLD TO COMPETE IN "PLAYING" AN IMAGINARY GUITAR.

In italy, there's a sport called "Palio," a historic bareback horse race held in Siena's Piazza del Campo twice a year.

The National Hollerin' Contest in the US celebrates the ancient art of hollering, or loud, prolonged yelling, used for communication in rural areas.

A Quidditch World Cup is held annually, inspired by the Harry Potter series, with teams on broomsticks playing a version of the magical game.

DOG SURFING IS AN ACTUAL COMPETITIVE SPORT, WITH EVENTS HELD IN CALIFORNIA, HAWAII, AND AUSTRALIA.

CHESS BOXING ORIGINATED IN BERLIN IN 2003 AND INVOLVES 11 ALTERNATING ROUNDS OF CHESS AND BOXING.

IN AUSTRALIA, THEY HOLD "COCKROACH RACING" EVERY AUSTRALIA DAY, WHERE COCKROACHES RACE FOR THE CHAMPIONSHIP TITLE.

THE "FISTBALL" WORLD CHAMPIONSHIPS ARE HELD FOR A GAME THAT RESEMBLES VOLLEYBALL BUT IS PLAYED WITH FISTS INSTEAD OF HANDS.

IN "KABADDI," PLAYERS MUST CONTINUOUSLY CHANT THE WORD "KABADDI" WHILE TRYING TO TAG AND ESCAPE THEIR OPPONENTS.

IN THE "WORLD BOG SNORKELING CHAMPIONSHIP" IN WALES, COMPETITORS SWIM THROUGH MUDDY, WATER-FILLED TRENCHES.

"UNDERWATER ICE HOCKEY" IS PLAYED UNDER A FROZEN LAKE OR SWIMMING POOL WITH PUCKS THAT SINK.

THE UK HOSTS AN ANNUAL "WORM CHARMING" CHAMPIONSHIP, WHERE COMPETITORS TRY TO LURE WORMS TO THE SURFACE USING VIBRATIONS.

COMPETITIVE STONE SKIPPING IS A SPORT WHERE PLAYERS COMPETE TO SEE WHO CAN MAKE A STONE SKIP THE MOST TIMES ACROSS WATER.

"BUS PULLING" IS A SPORT WHERE CONTESTANTS USE ONLY THEIR STRENGTH TO PULL A BUS AS FAR AS POSSIBLE.

PATO, ARGENTINA'S NATIONAL SPORT, IS A MIX OF POLO AND BASKETBALL AND IS PLAYED ON HORSEBACK.

IN SCOTLAND, THEY PLAY "CABER TOSS," A SPORT WHERE PARTICIPANTS TOSS A LARGE LOG END-OVER-END.

CARDBOARD BOAT RACING IS EXACTLY WHAT IT SOUNDS LIKE: RACING IN BOATS MADE ENTIRELY OF CARDBOARD.

IN CANADA, PEOPLE RACE OUTHOUSES ON WHEELS DURING THE ANNUAL "OUTHOUSE RACES."

THE FIRST KNOWN GAME OF BASKETBALL WAS PLAYED WITH A SOCCER BALL AND TWO PEACH BASKETS AS GOALS.

THE SPORT OF "ROLLER DERBY" ORIGINATED IN THE 1930S AS A COMBINATION OF RACING AND PHYSICAL COMBAT ON ROLLER SKATES.

SPEED CLIMBING IS A COMPETITIVE SPORT WHERE CLIMBERS RACE TO THE TOP OF A CLIMBING WALL IN RECORD TIME.

IN "ZORBING," PARTICIPANTS ROLL DOWN A HILL IN A GIANT INFLATABLE BALL.

IN 2010, THE WORLD RECORD FOR THE LONGEST PAPER AIRPLANE FLIGHT WAS SET AT 226 FEET.

A SPORT CALLED "SEPAK TAKRAW" IS LIKE VOLLEYBALL, BUT YOU CAN ONLY USE YOUR FEET, HEAD, KNEES, AND CHEST TO HIT THE BALL.

COMPETITIVE BEARD AND MUSTACHE CONTESTS JUDGE FACIAL HAIR ON STYLE, CREATIVITY, AND LENGTH.

TUG-OF-WAR IS STILL A COMPETITIVE SPORT TODAY, WITH INTERNATIONAL COMPETITIONS HELD ANNUALLY.

KITE FIGHTING, POPULAR IN INDIA AND PAKISTAN, IS A COMPETITIVE SPORT WHERE PARTICIPANTS TRY TO CUT EACH OTHER'S KITE STRINGS WITH THEIR OWN.

THE WORLD ICE GOLF CHAMPIONSHIP IS PLAYED ON A COURSE MADE ENTIRELY OF ICE IN GREENLAND.

THERE IS A MARBLE RACING WORLD CHAMPIONSHIP WHERE COMPETITORS RACE MARBLES DOWN ELABORATE COURSES.

"PANJAT PINANG" IS AN INDONESIAN SPORT WHERE PARTICIPANTS CLIMB GREASED POLES TO RETRIEVE PRIZES.

THE "WORLD PEA SHOOTING CHAMPIONSHIP" HAS BEEN HELD ANNUALLY IN ENGLAND SINCE 1971.

THE "UNICYCLE WORLD CHAMPIONSHIPS" FEATURE EVENTS LIKE UNICYCLE BASKETBALL, UNICYCLE HOCKEY, AND LONG-DISTANCE RACES.

THE "PUMPKIN REGATTA" IS A SPORT WHERE PARTICIPANTS RACE IN GIANT HOLLOW

THE "PUMPKIN REGATTA" IS A SPORT WHERE PARTICIPANTS RACE IN GIANT HOLLOWED-OUT PUMPKINS ACROSS A BODY OF WATER.

THE SPORT OF "BOG SNORKELING" INVOLVES COMPETITORS SWIMMING THROUGH A PEAT BOG WHILE WEARING SNORKELS AND FLIPPERS.

"DOG FRISBEE" IS A PROFESSIONAL SPORT WITH ITS OWN WORLD CHAMPIONSHIPS, WHERE DOGS AND THEIR OWNERS COMPETE IN FRISBEE-CATCHING CONTESTS.

IN AUSTRALIA, "BEER CAN REGATTAS" INVOLVE RACES WITH BOATS MADE ENTIRELY OF EMPTY BEER CANS.

"SPEEDCUBING" IS A COMPETITIVE SPORT WHERE CONTESTANTS SOLVE RUBIK'S CUBES AS FAST AS POSSIBLE.

IN "OCTOPUSH," OR UNDERWATER HOCKEY, TEAMS OF SIX USE TINY STICKS TO PUSH A PUCK ALONG THE BOTTOM OF A SWIMMING POOL.

QUOKKA SOCCER IS A SPORT UNIQUE TO AUSTRALIA, WHERE PLAYERS KICK A BALL WHILE AVOIDING QUOKKAS, SMALL MARSUPIALS, ON THE FIELD.

IN "MUD OLYMPICS," PARTICIPANTS COMPETE IN VARIOUS SPORTS—LIKE SOCCER AND VOLLEYBALL—BUT IN DEEP MUD.

IN "CHESS BOXING," COMPETITORS MUST WIN BY EITHER CHECKMATE OR KNOCKOUT.

THE "WORLD'S LONGEST CRICKET MATCH" WAS PLAYED IN ENGLAND IN 1939, LASTING NINE DAYS.

THE "HURLING WORLD CHAMPIONSHIP" FEATURES THE IRISH SPORT OF HURLING, OFTEN CONSIDERED ONE OF THE FASTEST GAMES ON GRASS.

IN JAPAN, "SUMO WRESTLING" TOURNAMENTS ARE HELD IN OUTDOOR TEMPLES, WITH MATCHES OFTEN LASTING LESS THAN 30 SECONDS.

"HORSEBALL" IS A SPORT SIMILAR TO BASKETBALL BUT PLAYED ON HORSEBACK.

IN "UNDERWATER FOOTBALL," PLAYERS USE A BALL FILLED WITH WATER AND PLAY A VERSION OF AMERICAN FOOTBALL IN A SWIMMING POOL.

"BANANA TOSSING" IS A SPORT IN WHICH COMPETITORS THROW BANANAS AS FAR AS POSSIBLE WITHOUT THEM BREAKING.

"CHESS BOXING" ORIGINATED AS AN ART PERFORMANCE BUT LATER BECAME A GLOBAL SPORT WITH A WORLD CHAMPIONSHIP.

THE LONGEST MARATHON PLAYING "TABLE TENNIS" LASTED 132 HOURS AND TOOK PLACE IN 1978.

"ROCK PAPER SCISSORS" HAS ITS OWN INTERNATIONAL TOURNAMENTS, COMPLETE WITH OFFICIAL RULES AND REFEREES.

THERE IS A "WORLD BEARD AND MOUSTACHE CHAMPIONSHIP" WHERE COMPETITORS' FACIAL HAIR IS JUDGED ON CREATIVITY AND STYLE.

IN "PLUNGE FOR DISTANCE," A COMPETITOR SWIMS UNDERWATER WITHOUT MOVING ANY LIMBS AND LETS MOMENTUM TAKE THEM AS FAR AS POSSIBLE.

"TUNA TOSSING" IS AN AUSTRALIAN SPORT WHERE COMPETITORS TOSS A FROZEN TUNA AS FAR AS THEY CAN.

IN "FOOTGOLF," PLAYERS KICK A SOCCER BALL INTO A SERIES OF HOLES ON A GOLF COURSE IN AS FEW SHOTS AS POSSIBLE.

THE "WORLD PILLOW FIGHTING CHAMPIONSHIP" FEATURES COMPETITORS HITTING EACH OTHER WITH PILLOWS WHILE TRYING TO KNOCK OPPONENTS OFF THEIR FEET.

"UNDERWATER RUGBY" IS PLAYED WITH A SINKING BALL IN A DEEP POOL, WHERE PLAYERS TRY TO SCORE GOALS IN SUBMERGED NETS.

THE "WORLD BATHTUBBING CHAMPIONSHIPS" INVOLVE RACING BATHTUBS DOWN A RIVER.

IN "CONKER FIGHTING," COMPETITORS USE CHESTNUTS (CONKERS) ON STRINGS TO SMASH EACH OTHER'S CONKER, WITH THE LAST INTACT CHESTNUT WINNING.

"HEADIS" IS A SPORT THAT COMBINES TABLE TENNIS AND SOCCER, WHERE PLAYERS USE THEIR HEADS TO HIT THE BALL ACROSS THE TABLE.

"MUGGLE QUIDDITCH" IS A NON-MAGICAL ADAPTATION OF THE HARRY POTTER SPORT, WITH PLAYERS RUNNING ON BROOMSTICKS WHILE PLAYING A MIX OF HANDBALL AND DODGEBALL.

THE "WORLD SNAIL RACING CHAMPIONSHIPS" FEATURES SNAILS COMPETING TO CROSS THE FINISH LINE FIRST.

"MAN VS. HORSE" IS A RACE HELD ANNUALLY IN WALES, WHERE HUMANS RACE HORSES ACROSS ROUGH TERRAIN. HUMANS HAVE WON IT TWICE!

"UNICYCLE SUMO" IS A COMPETITIVE SPORT WHERE PARTICIPANTS RIDE UNICYCLES AND TRY TO PUSH EACH OTHER OUT OF A RING, SIMILAR TO TRADITIONAL SUMO WRESTLING.

HiLLARiOUS

HiSTORY

102 FACTS

NAPOLEON WAS ONCE ATTACKED BY A HORDE OF BUNNIES DURING A HUNTING TRIP. THE BUNNIES OVERPOWERED HIM AND HIS MEN.

CLEOPATRA LIVED CLOSER IN TIME TO THE MOON LANDING THAN TO THE CONSTRUCTION OF THE GREAT PYRAMIDS.

IN 1923, JOCKEY FRANK HAYES WON A HORSE RACE DESPITE BEING DEAD. HE SUFFERED A HEART ATTACK MID-RACE BUT REMAINED IN THE SADDLE AS HIS HORSE CROSSED THE FINISH LINE.

THE SHORTEST WAR IN HISTORY WAS BETWEEN BRITAIN AND ZANZIBAR IN 1896. ZANZIBAR SURRENDERED AFTER JUST 38 MINUTES.

IN 1386, A PIG WAS PUT ON TRIAL IN FRANCE FOR MURDERING A CHILD— AND IT WAS FOUND GUILTY AND HANGED.

PRESIDENT ANDREW JACKSON HAD A PARROT THAT WAS EJECTED FROM HIS FUNERAL FOR SWEARING TOO MUCH.

IN 1917, A SILENT FILM ACTOR SUED ANOTHER MAN FOR SLAPPING HIM ON STAGE... WITH A PAIR OF GLOVES. THE COURT CASE WAS DISMISSED FOR BEING TOO RIDICULOUS.

IN 1866, THE KING OF BELGIUM OFFERED TO SELL HIS COUNTRY TO FRANCE, BUT NAPOLEON III DECLINED.

DURING THE VICTORIAN ERA, IT WAS FASHIONABLE TO TAKE PICTURES WITH DEAD RELATIVES, PROPPING THEM UP TO LOOK ALIVE IN THE PHOTO.

A FRENCH WOMAN ONCE SURVIVED BOTH THE SINKING OF THE TITANIC AND THE SINKING OF ITS SISTER SHIP, THE BRITANNIC.

IN 1912, A DOG NAMED BOBBIE WALKED 2,500 MILES ACROSS THE U.S. TO RETURN HOME AFTER BEING ACCIDENTALLY LEFT BEHIND BY HIS FAMILY ON VACATION.

PETER THE GREAT OF RUSSIA HAD A THING FOR TEETH. HE ONCE PULLED OUT A NOBLEMAN'S TOOTH HIMSELF TO PRACTICE DENTISTRY.

IN THE 1920S, THE SOVIET UNION TRIED TO BREED HUMANS WITH APES TO CREATE SUPERHUMAN SOLDIERS. FORTUNATELY, IT FAILED.

AT THE HEIGHT OF HIS FAME, NIKOLA TESLA FELL IN LOVE WITH A PIGEON.

IN ANCIENT EGYPT, SERVANTS WERE COVERED IN HONEY TO ATTRACT FLIES AWAY FROM THE PHARAOH.

KING GEORGE I OF ENGLAND DIDN'T SPEAK ENGLISH. HE WAS BORN AND RAISED IN GERMANY AND RULED ENGLAND FROM 1714 UNTIL HIS DEATH.

DURING WWII, THE BRITISH MILITARY USED INFLATABLE TANKS AND DUMMY PARATROOPERS TO TRICK THE GERMANS.

IN THE 16TH CENTURY, A COURT JESTER NAMED TRIBOULET WAS GRANTED A PARDON ON THE CONDITION THAT HE COULD CHOOSE HOW TO DIE. HE CHOSE "OLD AGE."

THE INVENTOR OF THE MODERN TOILET, THOMAS CRAPPER, DID NOT INVENT IT BUT POPULARIZED IT. THE WORD "CRAP" EXISTED LONG BEFORE HIS NAME BECAME ASSOCIATED WITH IT.

IN 1325, TWO ITALIAN CITY-STATES WENT TO WAR OVER A STOLEN BUCKET. THE "WAR OF THE OAKEN BUCKET" RESULTED IN THOUSANDS OF CASUALTIES.

IN 1788, THE AUSTRIAN ARMY ACCIDENTALLY ATTACKED ITSELF DURING A BATTLE, LEADING TO 10,000 CASUALTIES.

A CHICKEN NAMED MIKE LIVED FOR 18 MONTHS WITHOUT A HEAD AFTER A FAILED DECAPITATION ATTEMPT IN 1945.

RONALD REAGAN ONCE WORKED AS A LIFEGUARD AND SAVED 77 PEOPLE FROM DROWNING BEFORE HE BECAME PRESIDENT.

IN 1911, FRANCE LEGALLY GAVE THE MONA LISA A "DAY OFF" FROM THE LOUVRE SO IT COULD "REST" AFTER IT WAS RECOVERED FROM BEING STOLEN.

ROMAN EMPEROR GAIUS, ALSO KNOWN AS CALIGULA, ONCE DECLARED WAR ON NEPTUNE, THE GOD OF THE SEA, AND ORDERED HIS SOLDIERS TO ATTACK THE WAVES WITH SPEARS.

THE FIRST BOMB DROPPED BY THE ALLIES ON BERLIN DURING WWII KILLED THE ONLY ELEPHANT IN THE BERLIN ZOO.

A MAN NAMED TIMOTHY DEXTER WAS SO WEALTHY, HE ONCE FAKED HIS OWN DEATH JUST TO SEE WHO WOULD COME TO HIS FUNERAL—AND THEN SCOLDED THE MOURNERS FOR NOT BEING MORE UPSET.

IN 1923, JOCKEY FRANK HAYES WON A RACE DESPITE DYING MID-RACE. HIS HORSE CROSSED THE FINISH LINE WITH HIS LIFELESS BODY STILL IN THE SADDLE.

HENRY VIII'S WIVES WERE OFTEN GIFTED WITH PET MONKEYS. THE PETS WERE TRAINED TO EAT MEALS AT THE ROYAL TABLE.

IN 1493, COLUMBUS THOUGHT HE SAW MERMAIDS. THEY WERE ACTUALLY MANATEES.

DURING THE GREAT EMU WAR OF 1932, THE AUSTRALIAN MILITARY LOST A BATTLE AGAINST AN ARMY OF EMUS.

KING TUTANKHAMUN'S DAGGER WAS MADE FROM METEORITE IRON.

IN 1977, THE COUNTRY OF AUSTRALIA LOST A PRIME MINISTER. HAROLD HOLT WENT SWIMMING AND WAS NEVER SEEN AGAIN.

ABRAHAM LINCOLN WAS A LICENSED BARTENDER. HE CO-OWNED A SALOON IN ILLINOIS BEFORE HIS POLITICAL CAREER TOOK OFF.

THE BRITISH ONCE TRIED TO TAX WINDOWS. THIS LED MANY PEOPLE TO BRICK UP THEIR WINDOWS TO AVOID PAYING THE TAX.

IN 1838, EDGAR ALLAN POE WROTE A STORY ABOUT FOUR SHIPWRECKED SAILORS WHO RESORTED TO CANNIBALISM. FORTY-SIX YEARS LATER, THIS EXACT SCENARIO PLAYED OUT IN REAL LIFE.

THE SHORTEST-REIGNING POPE IN HISTORY, POPE URBAN VII, REIGNED FOR JUST 13 DAYS BEFORE DYING OF MALARIA.

IN ANCIENT ROME, URINE WAS USED AS MOUTHWASH BECAUSE THE AMMONIA CLEANED TEETH.

WINSTON CHURCHILL'S MOTHER WAS BORN IN BROOKLYN, NEW YORK, MAKING HER THE FIRST AMERICAN MOTHER OF A BRITISH PRIME MINISTER.

IN 1916, THE ALLIED FORCES DROPPED PAMPHLETS ON GERMANY OFFERING FREE BEER TO ANY SOLDIERS WHO SURRENDERED.

THE FIRST KNOWN "YO MAMA" JOKE WAS FOUND ON A 3,500-YEAR-OLD BABYLONIAN TABLET.

IN 1821, GREEK SOLDIERS USED CATS TO DEFEAT AN OTTOMAN ARMY THAT WAS TERRIFIED OF CATS DUE TO A LOCAL SUPERSTITION.

THOMAS EDISON ELECTROCUTED AN ELEPHANT NAMED TOPSY IN 1903 TO DEMONSTRATE THE DANGERS OF ALTERNATING CURRENT (AC) ELECTRICITY.

IN 1835, THE NEW YORK SUN RAN A HOAX ARTICLE CLAIMING ASTRONOMERS HAD DISCOVERED LIFE ON THE MOON. PEOPLE BELIEVED IT FOR WEEKS.

PRESIDENT JAMES GARFIELD COULD WRITE LATIN WITH ONE HAND AND GREEK WITH THE OTHER, SIMULTANEOUSLY.

A BATTLE BETWEEN THE FRENCH AND THE OTTOMANS WAS POSTPONED IN 1547 DUE TO BAD WEATHER... SPECIFICALLY, BECAUSE THE CLOUDS RESEMBLED GIANT HORSES.

CATHERINE THE GREAT OF RUSSIA HAD A LIFE-SIZE REPLICA OF HER LOVER'S HEAD MADE FROM SOLID GOLD.

DURING THE 1904 OLYMPICS, MARATHON RUNNERS DRANK RAT POISON AND BRANDY TO BOOST THEIR PERFORMANCE.

MARIE ANTOINETTE'S FINAL WORDS BEFORE BEING GUILLOTINED WERE, "PARDON ME, SIR, I DID NOT MEAN TO DO IT," AFTER SHE ACCIDENTALLY STEPPED ON HER EXECUTIONER'S FOOT.

IN 1938, TWO RIVAL PALEONTOLOGISTS BLEW UP EACH OTHER'S FOSSIL SITES WITH DYNAMITE IN AN ATTEMPT TO PREVENT THEIR OPPONENT FROM MAKING DISCOVERIES.

WHEN POPE GREGORY IX DECLARED WAR ON CATS, IT LED TO AN INCREASE IN THE RAT POPULATION, WHICH CONTRIBUTED TO THE SPREAD OF THE BLACK PLAGUE.

THOMAS JEFFERSON KEPT PET MOCKINGBIRDS IN THE WHITE HOUSE, AND ONE OF THEM, NAMED "DICK," WAS KNOWN FOR SINGING WHILE SITTING ON HIS SHOULDER.

GEORGE WASHINGTON'S TEETH WEREN'T MADE OF WOOD. THEY WERE ACTUALLY MADE FROM HIPPOPOTAMUS IVORY AND OTHER HUMAN TEETH.

IN 1839, KING LOUIS PHILIPPE OF FRANCE ONCE RECEIVED A GIANT WHEEL OF CHEESE AS A GIFT FROM A RURAL TOWN. THE CHEESE WEIGHED OVER 1,000 POUNDS.

IN 1770, BRITISH PARLIAMENT PASSED A LAW THAT MADE IT ILLEGAL FOR WOMEN TO WEAR MAKEUP BECAUSE IT WAS THOUGHT TO BE WITCHCRAFT.

IN 1912, OLYMPIC ATHLETE JIM THORPE'S SHOES WERE STOLEN JUST BEFORE HIS EVENT. HE FOUND TWO MISMATCHED SHOES IN THE TRASH AND WORE THEM TO WIN TWO GOLD MEDALS.

PRESIDENT JOHN QUINCY ADAMS ENJOYED SKINNY-DIPPING IN THE POTOMAC RIVER EVERY MORNING.

ALBERT EINSTEIN WAS OFFERED THE PRESIDENCY OF ISRAEL IN 1952, BUT HE DECLINED.

ONE OF THE OLDEST PRESERVED HUMAN BRAINS IS OVER 2,600 YEARS OLD AND WAS FOUND IN A BOG IN ENGLAND.

THE FAMOUS VIKING, ERIK THE RED, WAS SO NAMED BECAUSE OF HIS RED HAIR—AND HIS HOT TEMPER.

THE INVENTOR OF THE PRINGLES CAN, FRED BAUR, HAD HIS ASHES BURIED IN A PRINGLES CAN.

IN THE 1700S, PEOPLE IN FRANCE BELIEVED EATING TOMATOES WOULD TURN THEM INTO WEREWOLVES.

IN 1923, HITLER'S ATTEMPTED COUP IN MUNICH, KNOWN AS THE BEER HALL PUTSCH, WAS THWARTED IN PART BY TRAFFIC JAMS.

THE WORLD'S LONGEST HICCUPING SPREE LASTED 68 YEARS, STARTING IN 1922.

THE LEANING TOWER OF PISA WAS NEVER INTENDED TO LEAN. THE BUILDERS JUST DIDN'T REALIZE THE SOIL UNDER IT WAS TOO SOFT.

HENRY VIII SPENT THE MODERN EQUIVALENT OF $18 MILLION ON A NEW YEAR'S PARTY IN 1541.

IN 1830, THE BRITISH PARLIAMENT DECIDED TO CHANGE THE DATE OF CHRISTMAS TO MATCH THE JULIAN CALENDAR, BUT THEY GAVE UP AFTER THREE DAYS BECAUSE NO ONE CARED.

IN 1936, A BABY WAS ELECTED MAYOR OF A SMALL TOWN IN TEXAS. HE WAS 11 MONTHS OLD.

THERE WAS A PLAN TO ASSASSINATE FIDEL CASTRO BY GIVING HIM AN EXPLODING CIGAR.

IN 1920, BABE RUTH ONCE HIT A HOME RUN THAT TRAVELED 587 FEET.

DURING PROHIBITION, MOONSHINERS WOULD WEAR COW SHOES WITH WOODEN BLOCKS SHAPED LIKE HOOVES TO AVOID LEAVING FOOTPRINTS.

ANCIENT ROMAN SURGEONS OFTEN USED GLADIATOR BLOOD AS A TREATMENT FOR EPILEPSY.

CHARLES DARWIN ATE EVERY ANIMAL HE EVER DISCOVERED.

IN 1807, THE U.S. CONGRESS PASSED A LAW PROHIBITING DUELS IN WASHINGTON, D.C., BUT DUELING REMAINED POPULAR ELSEWHERE.

IN 1859, THE U.S. AND THE UK ALMOST WENT TO WAR OVER A PIG IN THE PACIFIC NORTHWEST. THE CONFLICT, KNOWN AS THE PIG WAR, WAS RESOLVED WITHOUT VIOLENCE.

IN 16TH CENTURY EUROPE, SOME WOMEN WORE DRESSES WITH CAGE-LIKE STRUCTURES THAT STRETCHED 18 FEET ACROSS.

IN 1872, THE CREW OF THE MARY CELESTE VANISHED WITHOUT A TRACE, LEAVING THE SHIP PERFECTLY INTACT AND STILL SAILING.

DURING THE AMERICAN CIVIL WAR, SOLDIERS ON BOTH SIDES WOULD SOMETIMES EXCHANGE COFFEE AND TOBACCO ACROSS BATTLE LINES DURING CEASEFIRES.

IN ANCIENT CHINA, PEOPLE WOULD EAT TEA LEAVES COMPRESSED INTO BRICKS AS CURRENCY.

IN 1938, BRITISH PRIME MINISTER NEVILLE CHAMBERLAIN GIFTED ADOLF HITLER A TOY BULLDOG AS A PEACE OFFERING.

IN THE 18TH CENTURY, WOMEN IN FRANCE WOULD WEAR HUGE WIGS WITH LIVE BIRDS AND OTHER ANIMALS PERCHED IN THEM.

DURING THE VICTORIAN ERA, PEOPLE BELIEVED THAT MUMMIES HAD HEALING POWERS, SO GROUND-UP MUMMIES WERE SOLD AS MEDICINE.

ALEXANDER THE GREAT'S BODY WAS REPORTEDLY PRESERVED IN HONEY AFTER HIS DEATH.

THE AZTECS USED CACAO BEANS AS CURRENCY.

THE FIRST RECORDED "SELFIE" WAS TAKEN BY ROBERT CORNELIUS IN 1839.

THE FIRST SPEEDING TICKET WAS ISSUED IN 1896 TO A DRIVER GOING 8 MPH.

IN 1714, THE BRITISH GOVERNMENT OFFERED A CASH PRIZE TO ANYONE WHO COULD ACCURATELY DETERMINE A SHIP'S LONGITUDE. IT TOOK 58 YEARS FOR SOMEONE TO WIN.

DURING THE 1904 OLYMPICS IN ST. LOUIS, ONE MARATHON RUNNER TOOK A NAP IN THE MIDDLE OF THE RACE AND STILL FINISHED FOURTH.

IN 1856, AN AUSTRIAN TAILOR NAMED FRANZ REICHELT JUMPED OFF THE EIFFEL TOWER WEARING A PARACHUTE SUIT HE INVENTED. IT DIDN'T WORK.

MOZART ONCE COMPOSED A PIECE OF MUSIC CALLED "LECK MICH IM ARSCH," WHICH TRANSLATES TO "KISS MY BUTT."

QUEEN VICTORIA SURVIVED AT LEAST SEVEN ASSASSINATION ATTEMPTS.

DURING WWII, THE BRITISH GOVERNMENT CONSIDERED RELEASING GLUE-COVERED BALLOONS OVER GERMANY TO CAUSE CHAOS.

THOMAS JEFFERSON INVENTED THE SWIVEL CHAIR.

IN 1916, AN ELEPHANT NAMED MARY WAS PUBLICLY EXECUTED BY HANGING IN TENNESSEE AFTER KILLING HER TRAINER.

AT THE AGE OF 9, LOUIS XIV BECAME KING OF FRANCE BUT DIDN'T START RULING UNTIL HE WAS 13 BECAUSE HE DIDN'T WANT TO LEAVE HIS TOYS.

GENGHIS KHAN'S DESCENDANTS MAKE UP 8% OF THE MEN LIVING IN THE REGION FORMERLY RULED BY HIS EMPIRE.

BENJAMIN FRANKLIN ONCE WROTE AN ESSAY TITLED "FART PROUDLY," URGING SCIENTIFIC RESEARCH ON FLATULENCE.

IN 1839, "LAUGHING GAS" WAS USED AS A PARTY DRUG BY WEALTHY PEOPLE IN THE UK.

PRESIDENT WILLIAM HOWARD TAFT ONCE GOT STUCK IN THE WHITE HOUSE BATHTUB AND HAD TO BE RESCUED BY STAFF.

IN ANCIENT GREECE, WEARING A FAKE BEARD WAS CONSIDERED A SERIOUS CRIME.

IN 1924, A LABRADOR RETRIEVER NAMED BUDDY BECAME THE FIRST SEEING-EYE DOG IN THE U.S. BUT BEFORE HIS NOBLE CAREER, BUDDY HAD BEEN TRAINED TO RETRIEVE BEER FROM THE FRIDGE FOR HIS OWNER.

ABRAHAM LINCOLN WAS A WRESTLING CHAMPION AND ONLY LOST ONE MATCH IN HIS CAREER.

NATURE GONE NUTS

NUTS

101 FACTS

WOMBAT POOP IS CUBE-SHAPED.
SCIENTISTS THINK THIS HELPS IT STAY
IN PLACE AND MARK TERRITORY.

A GROUP OF FLAMINGOS IS CALLED A
"FLAMBOYANCE."

KOALAS SLEEP FOR UP TO 22 HOURS A
DAY. THEY'RE BASICALLY NATURE'S
LAZIEST ANIMAL.

SHARKS HAVE BEEN AROUND LONGER THAN TREES. THEY'VE EXISTED FOR OVER 400 MILLION YEARS!

SLOTHS ARE SO SLOW THAT ALGAE GROWS ON THEIR FUR, GIVING THEM A GREEN TINT.

SEA OTTERS HOLD HANDS WHILE SLEEPING SO THEY DON'T DRIFT APART IN THE WATER.

THERE ARE MORE FAKE FLAMINGOS IN THE WORLD THAN REAL ONES.

AN OSTRICH'S EYE IS BIGGER THAN ITS BRAIN.

THE MANTIS SHRIMP HAS THE FASTEST PUNCH IN THE ANIMAL KINGDOM. ITS STRIKE CAN BREAK AQUARIUM GLASS.

COWS HAVE BEST FRIENDS AND GET STRESSED WHEN THEY ARE SEPARATED.

THE IMMORTAL JELLYFISH CAN REVERT TO ITS JUVENILE FORM AFTER REACHING ADULTHOOD, ESSENTIALLY LIVING FOREVER—UNLESS SOMETHING EATS IT.

MALE SEAHORSES, NOT FEMALES, ARE THE ONES THAT CARRY AND GIVE BIRTH TO THEIR BABIES.

A SINGLE ELEPHANT TOOTH CAN WEIGH AS MUCH AS 9 POUNDS.

BUTTERFLIES TASTE WITH THEIR FEET.

POLAR BEARS HAVE BLACK SKIN UNDER THEIR WHITE FUR TO HELP ABSORB HEAT FROM THE SUN.

THE HEART OF A BLUE WHALE IS SO LARGE THAT A HUMAN COULD SWIM THROUGH ITS ARTERIES.

SOME SPECIES OF ANT CAN FORM LIVING RAFTS DURING FLOODS BY LINKING TOGETHER, KEEPING THEIR QUEEN SAFE AND DRY IN THE CENTER.

THE FEMALE BLANKET OCTOPUS CAN DETACH ONE OF HER ARMS TO DISTRACT PREDATORS, AND SHE CAN REGROW IT LATER.

THE GREENLAND SHARK CAN LIVE FOR OVER 500 YEARS, MAKING IT THE LONGEST-LIVING VERTEBRATE ON EARTH.

COWS MOO IN ACCENTS. THEIR MOO SOUNDS DIFFERENT DEPENDING ON WHERE THEY ARE FROM.

THE LOUDEST SOUND EVER RECORDED IN NATURE WAS THE KRAKATOA VOLCANIC ERUPTION IN 1883, WHICH WAS HEARD OVER 3,000 MILES AWAY.

KANGAROOS CAN'T WALK BACKWARD.

THE STAR-NOSED MOLE CAN DETECT, CATCH, AND EAT ITS PREY IN UNDER 0.2 SECONDS, MAKING IT THE FASTEST-EATING MAMMAL.

GIRAFFES HAVE THE SAME NUMBER OF NECK VERTEBRAE AS HUMANS—JUST 7. BUT GIRAFFE VERTEBRAE ARE ABOUT 10 INCHES LONG EACH.

A GROUP OF CROWS IS CALLED A "MURDER," BUT A GROUP OF ZEBRAS IS CALLED A "DAZZLE."

ELEPHANTS ARE THE ONLY ANIMALS THAT CAN'T JUMP.

THE PLATYPUS DOESN'T HAVE A STOMACH; ITS ESOPHAGUS GOES STRAIGHT TO ITS INTESTINES.

PIGEONS CAN DO MATH. THEY'VE BEEN SHOWN TO UNDERSTAND ABSTRACT NUMERICAL CONCEPTS.

HONEY NEVER SPOILS. ARCHAEOLOGISTS HAVE FOUND POTS OF HONEY IN ANCIENT EGYPTIAN TOMBS THAT ARE STILL PERFECTLY EDIBLE.

SOME SPECIES OF DEEP-SEA FISH, LIKE THE BLACK DRAGONFISH, HAVE SEE-THROUGH SKIN.

FROGS CAN THROW UP THEIR ENTIRE STOMACHS, CLEAN THEM, AND SWALLOW THEM BACK DOWN.

THE AFRICAN LUNGFISH CAN SURVIVE OUT OF WATER FOR UP TO A YEAR BY BURROWING INTO THE MUD AND SECRETING A MUCOUS COCOON.

TARDIGRADES, ALSO KNOWN AS WATER BEARS, CAN SURVIVE IN EXTREME CONDITIONS, INCLUDING THE VACUUM OF SPACE.

THE AXOLOTL, A TYPE OF SALAMANDER, CAN REGROW ITS LIMBS, SPINE, AND EVEN PARTS OF ITS BRAIN.

A SNAIL CAN SLEEP FOR UP TO THREE YEARS AT A TIME IF CONDITIONS ARE NOT IDEAL.

PENGUINS PROPOSE TO THEIR MATES BY GIVING THEM A PEBBLE.

CROWS ARE SO INTELLIGENT THAT THEY CAN RECOGNIZE HUMAN FACES AND HOLD GRUDGES AGAINST INDIVIDUALS WHO HAVE WRONGED THEM.

THE MALE EMPEROR PENGUIN CAN GO WITHOUT EATING FOR OVER TWO MONTHS WHILE KEEPING AN EGG WARM IN FREEZING ANTARCTIC CONDITIONS.

THE NAKED MOLE RAT CAN LIVE UP TO 18 MINUTES WITHOUT OXYGEN.

THE PEACOCK MANTIS SHRIMP HAS THE MOST COMPLEX EYES IN THE ANIMAL KINGDOM, CAPABLE OF SEEING 12 COLOR CHANNELS, COMPARED TO HUMANS WHO CAN SEE ONLY THREE.

THE HAGFISH CAN PRODUCE ENOUGH SLIME TO FILL A BUCKET IN JUST MINUTES AS A DEFENSE MECHANISM.

AN ANT CAN LIFT UP TO 50 TIMES ITS BODY WEIGHT.

THE MIMIC OCTOPUS CAN IMITATE UP TO 15 DIFFERENT MARINE SPECIES, INCLUDING LIONFISH, FLATFISH, AND SEA SNAKES.

THE HORNED LIZARD CAN SHOOT BLOOD FROM ITS EYES TO SCARE OFF PREDATORS.

THE PEREGRINE FALCON IS THE FASTEST BIRD, DIVING AT SPEEDS OVER 240 MILES PER HOUR.

DOLPHINS HAVE BEEN OBSERVED USING PUFFERFISH TO GET "HIGH." THE PUFFERFISH'S TOXINS IN SMALL DOSES PRODUCE A NARCOTIC EFFECT.

TIGERS HAVE STRIPED SKIN, NOT JUST STRIPED FUR.

A RHINOCEROS' HORN IS MADE OF KERATIN—THE SAME SUBSTANCE AS HUMAN HAIR AND NAILS.

JELLYFISH HAVE BEEN AROUND FOR MORE THAN 500 MILLION YEARS, MAKING THEM OLDER THAN DINOSAURS.

SOME MALE SPIDERS TIE UP THEIR MATES BEFORE MATING TO AVOID BEING EATEN AFTERWARD.

ARMADILLOS CAN HOLD THEIR BREATH FOR UP TO SIX MINUTES AND ARE KNOWN TO WALK ALONG THE BOTTOM OF RIVERS.

THE PISTOL SHRIMP SNAPS ITS CLAW SO FAST IT CREATES A BUBBLE THAT BRIEFLY REACHES TEMPERATURES HOTTER THAN THE SURFACE OF THE SUN.

HIPPOS SWEAT A NATURAL SUNSCREEN THAT IS RED AND HELPS PREVENT INFECTIONS.

HORSES AND COWS CAN SLEEP STANDING UP, BUT THEY CAN ONLY DREAM WHEN LYING DOWN.

ALBATROSSES MATE FOR LIFE, AND IF ONE PARTNER DIES, THE OTHER MAY REMAIN SINGLE FOR THE REST OF ITS LIFE.

THE AYE-AYE LEMUR TAPS ON TREES WITH ITS LONG MIDDLE FINGER TO FIND INSECTS AND USES THE SAME FINGER TO EXTRACT THEM.

THE ELECTRIC EEL CAN PRODUCE A SHOCK OF UP TO 600 VOLTS, ENOUGH TO STUN A HORSE.

A SHRIMP'S HEART IS LOCATED IN ITS HEAD.

SLOTHS CAN SWIM THREE TIMES FASTER THAN THEY CAN MOVE ON LAND.

THE MIMIC OCTOPUS CAN CHANGE ITS COLOR, SHAPE, AND BEHAVIOR TO IMITATE MORE DANGEROUS ANIMALS LIKE SEA SNAKES OR LIONFISH.

SOME FROGS GLOW UNDER ULTRAVIOLET LIGHT, A PHENOMENON SCIENTISTS DISCOVERED BY ACCIDENT.

A GROUP OF PORCUPINES IS CALLED A "PRICKLE."

DRAGONFLIES CAN CATCH UP TO 95% OF THE PREY THEY HUNT, MAKING THEM ONE OF THE MOST EFFECTIVE PREDATORS IN THE ANIMAL KINGDOM.

THE MALE JACANA BIRD TAKES CARE OF THE EGGS AND CHICKS, WHILE THE FEMALE MATES WITH MULTIPLE MALES.

SOME SQUIRRELS FAKE-BURY THEIR FOOD TO TRICK OTHER ANIMALS WATCHING THEM.

COWS PRODUCE MORE MILK WHEN THEY LISTEN TO SLOW MUSIC.

THE BOMBARDIER BEETLE CAN SHOOT A BOILING HOT CHEMICAL SPRAY FROM ITS ABDOMEN TO DEFEND ITSELF.

A FLAMINGO CAN ONLY EAT WITH ITS HEAD UPSIDE DOWN.

THE PLATYPUS IS ONE OF THE FEW VENOMOUS MAMMALS, WITH MALES HAVING VENOMOUS SPURS ON THEIR HIND LEGS.

ANTS DON'T SLEEP. INSTEAD, THEY TAKE SHORT POWER NAPS THROUGHOUT THE DAY.

BEAVERS' TEETH NEVER STOP GROWING, SO THEY MUST GNAW ON WOOD TO KEEP THEM AT A MANAGEABLE LENGTH.

THE SLOW LORIS IS ONE OF THE ONLY VENOMOUS PRIMATES, DELIVERING VENOM THROUGH A BITE.

THERE'S A FUNGUS IN THE RAINFOREST THAT INFECTS ANTS, TURNING THEM INTO "ZOMBIES" BY CONTROLLING THEIR MOVEMENTS.

SOME SPECIES OF CORAL CAN PRODUCE THEIR OWN SUNSCREEN TO PROTECT THEMSELVES FROM UV RAYS.

THE HOATZIN, A BIRD FOUND IN SOUTH AMERICA, IS KNOWN AS THE "STINK BIRD" BECAUSE IT SMELLS LIKE COW MANURE DUE TO ITS UNIQUE DIGESTIVE SYSTEM.

THE MALE PROBOSCIS MONKEY HAS A LARGE NOSE, WHICH IS THOUGHT TO ATTRACT FEMALES.

OWLS DON'T HAVE EYEBALLS. THEIR EYES ARE TUBE-SHAPED AND HELD IN PLACE BY BONY STRUCTURES, SO THEY CAN'T MOVE THEM—HENCE THE NEED TO ROTATE THEIR HEADS.

THE BLUE WHALE'S TONGUE WEIGHS AS MUCH AS AN ELEPHANT.

OCTOPUSES HAVE NINE BRAINS—ONE CENTRAL BRAIN AND ONE FOR EACH ARM.

THE HAGFISH CAN TIE ITSELF INTO A KNOT TO ESCAPE PREDATORS OR CLEAN ITSELF.

THERE ARE MORE STARS IN THE UNIVERSE THAN GRAINS OF SAND ON ALL THE EARTH'S BEACHES COMBINED.

FEMALE BATS GIVE BIRTH WHILE HANGING UPSIDE DOWN AND CATCH THEIR BABIES IN THEIR WINGS AS THEY FALL.

SOME MOTHS DON'T HAVE MOUTHS AND LIVE ONLY LONG ENOUGH TO MATE.

THE SURINAM TOAD GIVES BIRTH THROUGH HOLES IN ITS BACK, WHERE THE EGGS DEVELOP INTO TADPOLES.

MALE ANGLERFISH FUSE TO THE FEMALE'S BODY FOR LIFE, LIVING AS A PARASITE WHILE SHE PROVIDES ALL THEIR NUTRIENTS.

CROCODILES CAN'T STICK OUT THEIR TONGUES.

A GROUP OF JELLYFISH IS CALLED A "SMACK."

THE NARWHAL'S TUSK IS ACTUALLY AN ELONGATED TOOTH.

A KANGAROO CAN'T FART. INSTEAD, IT RELEASES GASES THROUGH BELCHING.

A GIRAFFE'S TONGUE CAN BE UP TO 20 INCHES LONG AND IS USED TO GRAB LEAVES AND CLEAN ITS FACE.

THE GIANT PANDA SPENDS ABOUT 12 HOURS A DAY EATING BAMBOO.

WHEN THREATENED, SEA CUCUMBERS CAN EXPEL THEIR INTERNAL ORGANS AS A DEFENSE MECHANISM.

THE BLOOD OF HORSESHOE CRABS IS BLUE DUE TO ITS COPPER-BASED MOLECULES.

MALE EMPEROR PENGUINS LOSE UP TO HALF THEIR BODY WEIGHT WHILE INCUBATING THEIR EGGS.

THE PANGOLIN IS THE ONLY MAMMAL COMPLETELY COVERED IN SCALES.

WHEN SCARED, A TURKEY'S HEAD CAN CHANGE COLOR, FROM RED TO BLUE TO WHITE, DEPENDING ON ITS LEVEL OF EXCITEMENT OR STRESS.

ELEPHANTS CAN RECOGNIZE THEMSELVES IN A MIRROR, SHOWING SIGNS OF SELF-AWARENESS.

CROWS HAVE FUNERALS. WHEN ONE CROW DIES, OTHER CROWS WILL GATHER AROUND TO INVESTIGATE THE CAUSE OF DEATH.

THE KAKAPO, A FLIGHTLESS PARROT FROM NEW ZEALAND, CAN ONLY MATE WHEN THE TREE THAT PROVIDES ITS FOOD PRODUCES ENOUGH FRUIT, WHICH HAPPENS EVERY FEW YEARS.

THE SAND CAT CAN LIVE IN THE DESERT WITHOUT DRINKING WATER, GETTING ALL ITS MOISTURE FROM ITS PREY.

THE PINK FAIRY ARMADILLO IS THE SMALLEST ARMADILLO SPECIES AND LOOKS LIKE A REAL-LIFE POKEMON.

THE ALPINE IBEX, A TYPE OF WILD GOAT, IS SO GOOD AT CLIMBING THAT IT CAN SCALE NEAR-VERTICAL DAM WALLS TO LICK SALT DEPOSITS.

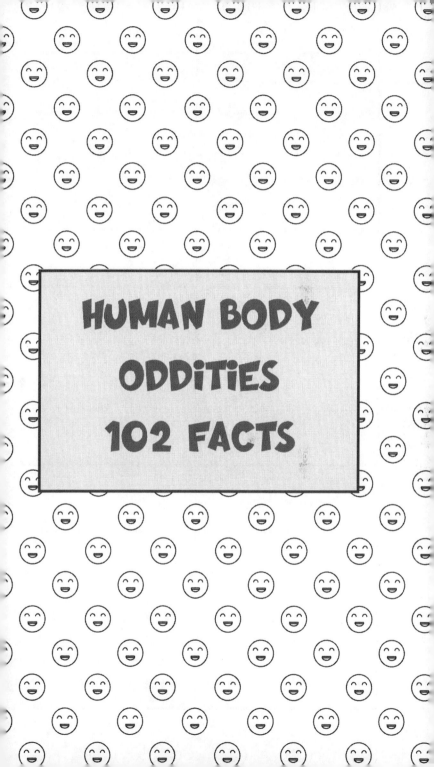

HUMAN BODY

ODDITIES

102 FACTS

THE HUMAN NOSE CAN REMEMBER OVER 50,000 DIFFERENT SCENTS.

YOU SHED ABOUT 40,000 SKIN CELLS EVERY MINUTE.

HUMAN BONES ARE ABOUT FIVE TIMES STRONGER THAN STEEL OF THE SAME DENSITY.

THE ONLY PART OF THE BODY THAT CAN'T REPAIR ITSELF IS THE TEETH.

YOUR BODY PRODUCES ABOUT A LITER OF MUCUS EVERY DAY.

HUMAN SALIVA CONTAINS A NATURAL PAINKILLER CALLED OPIORPHIN, WHICH IS SIX TIMES MORE POWERFUL THAN MORPHINE.

A PERSON CAN LIVE WITHOUT A LARGE PORTION OF THEIR LIVER. THE LIVER CAN REGENERATE ITSELF IF PART OF IT IS REMOVED.

THE ACID IN YOUR STOMACH IS STRONG ENOUGH TO DISSOLVE METAL.

THE AVERAGE PERSON'S SKIN WEIGHS TWICE AS MUCH AS THEIR BRAIN.

THE BRAIN OPERATES ON THE SAME
AMOUNT OF POWER AS A 10-WATT
LIGHT BULB.

YOU HAVE MORE BACTERIA IN YOUR
MOUTH THAN THERE ARE PEOPLE ON
EARTH.

WHEN YOU BLUSH, THE LINING OF
YOUR STOMACH ALSO TURNS RED.

THE HUMAN BODY CONTAINS ENOUGH FAT TO MAKE SEVEN BARS OF SOAP.

YOUR EARS AND NOSE NEVER STOP GROWING THROUGHOUT YOUR LIFE.

THE HUMAN EYE CAN DISTINGUISH ABOUT 10 MILLION DIFFERENT COLORS.

A SNEEZE CAN TRAVEL UP TO 100 MILES PER HOUR.

THE HUMAN BODY HAS OVER 600 MUSCLES, BUT THE STRONGEST MUSCLE BY WEIGHT IS THE MASSETER (JAW MUSCLE).

THE TONGUE IS THE ONLY MUSCLE IN YOUR BODY THAT IS ATTACHED AT JUST ONE END.

THE CORNEA, THE TRANSPARENT FRONT PART OF THE EYE, IS THE ONLY PART OF THE BODY THAT DOESN'T HAVE A BLOOD SUPPLY. IT GETS OXYGEN DIRECTLY FROM THE AIR.

THE HUMAN SKELETON IS COMPLETELY REPLACED EVERY 10 YEARS.

YOUR BRAIN USES ABOUT 20% OF YOUR BODY'S TOTAL OXYGEN AND ENERGY.

YOU ARE TALLER IN THE MORNING THAN AT NIGHT BECAUSE THE CARTILAGE IN YOUR SPINE COMPRESSES DURING THE DAY.

THE HUMAN BODY PRODUCES ENOUGH HEAT IN 30 MINUTES TO BOIL A GALLON OF WATER.

YOUR HEARTBEAT CHANGES AND MIMICS THE MUSIC YOU LISTEN TO.

YOUR FINGERPRINTS AREN'T JUST UNIQUE TO YOU; THEY ALSO HAVE A UNIQUE PATTERN ON EACH FINGER.

IT'S IMPOSSIBLE TO TICKLE YOURSELF BECAUSE YOUR BRAIN PREDICTS THE SENSATION.

THE AVERAGE HUMAN BODY HAS ABOUT 37.2 TRILLION CELLS.

HUMANS SHARE ABOUT 60% OF THEIR DNA WITH BANANAS.

BABIES HAVE ABOUT 300 BONES AT BIRTH, BUT BY ADULTHOOD, THEY ONLY HAVE 206 BECAUSE SOME BONES FUSE TOGETHER.

YOUR BODY CONTAINS ENOUGH IRON TO MAKE A 3-INCH NAIL.

THE BRAIN ITSELF DOESN'T FEEL PAIN. THAT'S WHY BRAIN SURGERIES CAN SOMETIMES BE PERFORMED WHILE THE PATIENT IS AWAKE.

IT'S IMPOSSIBLE TO HUM WHILE HOLDING YOUR NOSE. TRY IT!

THE FASTEST GROWING TISSUE IN THE HUMAN BODY IS HAIR.

YOUR STOMACH GETS A NEW LINING EVERY 3 TO 4 DAYS TO PREVENT IT FROM DIGESTING ITSELF.

THE AVERAGE HUMAN HEAD HAS ABOUT 100,000 HAIR FOLLICLES, AND EACH FOLLICLE CAN GROW ABOUT 20 INDIVIDUAL HAIRS IN A LIFETIME.

GOOSEBUMPS ARE A LEFTOVER REFLEX FROM WHEN HUMANS HAD MORE BODY HAIR AND NEEDED TO APPEAR LARGER TO SCARE OFF PREDATORS.

THE HUMAN BRAIN IS ABOUT 75% WATER.

THE LENGTH OF ALL THE BLOOD VESSELS IN THE HUMAN BODY IS ROUGHLY 60,000 MILES.

THE AVERAGE PERSON TAKES ABOUT 20,000 BREATHS PER DAY.

HUMAN BONES ARE CONSTANTLY BREAKING DOWN AND REBUILDING. IN FACT, YOU GET A COMPLETELY NEW SKELETON EVERY 7 TO 10 YEARS.

HUMANS SHED ABOUT 1.5 POUNDS OF SKIN EACH YEAR.

THE AVERAGE PERSON WILL PRODUCE ABOUT 25,000 QUARTS OF SALIVA IN THEIR LIFETIME—ENOUGH TO FILL TWO SWIMMING POOLS.

IT TAKES 17 MUSCLES TO SMILE AND 43 TO FROWN.

THE HUMAN EYE CAN FOCUS ON ABOUT 50 DIFFERENT OBJECTS PER SECOND.

THE BODY HAS OVER 72,000 NERVES.

YOUR LIVER CAN PERFORM OVER 500 DIFFERENT FUNCTIONS.

ON AVERAGE, HUMANS PRODUCE ENOUGH SWEAT TO FILL TWO BATHTUBS PER YEAR.

A BABY'S BODY IS MADE UP OF ABOUT 78% WATER, WHILE AN ADULT'S BODY IS ABOUT 60% WATER.

THE HUMAN BRAIN GENERATES ENOUGH ELECTRICITY TO POWER A SMALL LIGHT BULB.

THE SKIN IS THE LARGEST ORGAN IN THE HUMAN BODY AND MAKES UP ABOUT 15% OF YOUR BODY WEIGHT.

THE SMALL INTESTINE IS ABOUT 20 FEET LONG, BUT IT FITS INSIDE YOUR BODY BECAUSE IT'S COILED TIGHTLY.

YOUR TASTE BUDS ARE REPLACED
EVERY 10 TO 14 DAYS.

THE MUSCLES CONTROLLING YOUR
EYES MAKE THE FASTEST AND MOST
CONSISTENT MOVEMENTS IN THE
HUMAN BODY.

HUMAN TEETH ARE AS STRONG AS
SHARK TEETH.

THE AVERAGE HUMAN SPENDS ABOUT FIVE YEARS OF THEIR LIFE EATING.

EVERY HUMAN HAS A UNIQUE TONGUE PRINT, JUST LIKE FINGERPRINTS.

THE AVERAGE HUMAN SHEDS ABOUT 1.5 MILLION SKIN FLAKES PER HOUR.

YOUR BRAIN CONTAINS ABOUT 86 BILLION NERVE CELLS.

THE LIVER IS THE ONLY ORGAN THAT CAN REGENERATE ITSELF. YOU CAN LOSE UP TO 75% OF YOUR LIVER, AND IT WILL GROW BACK.

YOUR FINGERNAILS GROW FASTER ON YOUR DOMINANT HAND.

THE HUMAN HEART BEATS MORE THAN
100,000 TIMES A DAY.

A HEALTHY ADULT CAN PRODUCE
ENOUGH SALIVA IN A YEAR TO FILL
TWO MEDIUM-SIZED SWIMMING
POOLS.

A HUMAN SNEEZE CAN EXCEED THE
SPEED OF 100 MILES PER HOUR.

YOUR EYES BLINK ABOUT 20 TIMES PER MINUTE.

THE PINKY FINGER PROVIDES ABOUT 50% OF YOUR HAND'S STRENGTH.

HUMANS ARE THE ONLY ANIMALS THAT CRY EMOTIONAL TEARS.

A SINGLE HUMAN HAIR CAN SUPPORT UP TO 3.5 OUNCES OF WEIGHT.

THE TONGUE IS COVERED IN ABOUT 10,000 TASTE BUDS, AND EACH TASTE BUD HAS 50 TO 100 RECEPTOR CELLS.

THE HUMAN BODY HAS ENOUGH CARBON TO FILL ABOUT 9,000 PENCILS.

PEOPLE WITH BLUE EYES SHARE A COMMON ANCESTOR WITH EVERY OTHER BLUE-EYED PERSON ON EARTH.

YOUR EARS SECRETE MORE EARWAX WHEN YOU'RE AFRAID THAN WHEN YOU'RE CALM.

THE HEART PUMPS ABOUT 1.5 MILLION BARRELS OF BLOOD IN A LIFETIME.

THE ONLY MUSCLE THAT NEVER TIRES IS THE HEART.

EVERY MINUTE, YOUR BODY PRODUCES 300 MILLION NEW CELLS.

THE LEFT LUNG IS SMALLER THAN THE RIGHT LUNG TO MAKE ROOM FOR THE HEART.

THE FASTEST GROWING NAIL IS ON THE MIDDLE FINGER OF YOUR DOMINANT HAND.

A NEWBORN BABY HAS ABOUT ONE CUP OF BLOOD IN ITS ENTIRE BODY.

IF YOUR DNA WERE STRETCHED OUT, IT WOULD REACH TO THE MOON AND BACK ABOUT 17 TIMES.

YOUR BELLY BUTTON IS HOME TO THOUSANDS OF BACTERIA THAT FORM AN ECOSYSTEM AS COMPLEX AS A RAINFOREST.

MEN'S HEARTS BEAT ABOUT 10 TIMES PER MINUTE SLOWER THAN WOMEN'S HEARTS.

IT'S IMPOSSIBLE TO SWALLOW AND BREATHE AT THE SAME TIME.

YOUR BODY HAS MORE THAN 650 SKELETAL MUSCLES.

THE HUMAN BRAIN CAN SURVIVE FOR ABOUT FOUR TO SIX MINUTES WITHOUT OXYGEN BEFORE BRAIN DAMAGE OCCURS.

THE FOOT HAS 26 BONES, 33 JOINTS, AND MORE THAN 100 MUSCLES, TENDONS, AND LIGAMENTS.

THE HUMAN BODY IS CAPABLE OF PRODUCING ITS OWN ALCOHOL—SMALL AMOUNTS ARE MADE IN THE DIGESTIVE SYSTEM.

THE AVERAGE PERSON WALKS THE EQUIVALENT OF FIVE TIMES AROUND THE EARTH DURING THEIR LIFETIME.

THE SENSE OF SMELL IS CLOSELY LINKED TO MEMORY, WHICH IS WHY SMELLS OFTEN TRIGGER VIVID MEMORIES.

YOUR BONES ARE 31% WATER.

IF YOU DRINK TOO MUCH WATER TOO QUICKLY, YOU CAN SUFFER FROM A CONDITION CALLED "WATER INTOXICATION," WHICH CAN BE FATAL.

THE AVERAGE PERSON HAS ABOUT 100,000 HAIR FOLLICLES ON THEIR SCALP.

YOUR BODY LOSES UP TO 8% OF ITS WATER CONTENT EVERY DAY THROUGH SWEATING, BREATHING, AND URINATION.

HUMANS SHARE 98.8% OF THEIR DNA WITH CHIMPANZEES.

YOUR BODY IS CAPABLE OF PRODUCING ITS OWN VITAMIN D WITH SUNLIGHT EXPOSURE.

THE ONLY PART OF THE BODY THAT HAS NO BLOOD SUPPLY IS THE CORNEA OF THE EYE.

THE STRONGEST MUSCLE IN THE HUMAN BODY, POUND FOR POUND, IS THE TONGUE.

THE AVERAGE PERSON HAS 67 DIFFERENT SPECIES OF BACTERIA IN THEIR BELLY BUTTON.

YOUR BRAIN CAN STORE MORE INFORMATION THAN A COMPUTER WITH A CAPACITY OF ABOUT 2.5 PETABYTES, WHICH IS ABOUT A MILLION GIGABYTES.

YOUR BODY CONTAINS TRILLIONS OF MICROORGANISMS, OUTNUMBERING YOUR OWN CELLS BY ABOUT 10 TO 1.

THE AVERAGE PERSON WILL SPEND ABOUT 6 MONTHS OF THEIR LIFE WAITING FOR RED LIGHTS TO TURN GREEN.

THE AVERAGE ADULT HAS BETWEEN 2 AND 9 POUNDS OF BACTERIA IN THEIR BODY.

YOUR BODY REPLACES ABOUT 50 TO 70 BILLION CELLS EVERY DAY.

THE HUMAN BODY GLOWS IN THE DARK, BUT THE LIGHT EMITTED IS 1,000 TIMES WEAKER THAN WHAT OUR EYES CAN DETECT.

Made in United States
Troutdale, OR
12/15/2024

26587907R00089